LAUGH-OUT-LOUD JOKES

LAUGH-OUT-LOUD FOOD JOKES

CAITIE MCANENEY

WINDMILL BOOKS

Published in 2025 by Windmill Books, an Imprint of Rosen Publishing
2544 Clinton St., Buffalo, NY 14224

First Edition

Editor: Caitie McAneney
Book Design: Claire Zimmermann

Photo Credits: Cover, p.1 (child) PeopleImages.com - Yuri A/Shutterstock.com; series art (food illustrations) Nadzin/Shutterstock.com, (paper texture) OanaGherghe2/Shutterstock.com; p. 5 FILMME/Shutterstock.com; p. 7 Bigc Studio/Shutterstock.com; p. 9 Steve JM Hamilton/Shutterstock.com; p. 11 Brent Hofacker/Shutterstock.com; p. 13 David Pimborough/Shutterstock.com; p. 15 Pixel-Shot/Shutterstock.com; p. 16 (bread illustration) mything/Shutterstock.com; p. 17 Paul Cowan/Shutterstock.com; p. 18 (sandwich illustration) NikAndr/Shutterstock.com; p. 19 Flaffy/Shutterstock.com; p. 21 Aedka Studio/Shutterstock.com.

Some of the images in this book illustrate individuals who are models. The depictions do not imply actual situations or events.

Library of Congress Cataloging-in-Publication Data

Names: McAneney, Caitie, author.
Title: Laugh-out-loud food jokes / Caitie McAneney.
Description: Buffalo : Windmill Books, 2025. | Series: Laugh-out-loud jokes | Includes index.
Identifiers: LCCN 2024007964 (print) | LCCN 2024007965 (ebook) | ISBN 9781538396773 (library binding) | ISBN 9781538396766 (paperback) | ISBN 9781538396780 (ebook)
Subjects: LCSH: Food–Juvenile humor. | Wit and humor, Juvenile.
Classification: LCC PN6231.F66 M33 2024 (print) | LCC PN6231.F66 (ebook) | DDC 641.3002/07–dc23/eng/20240317
LC record available at https://lccn.loc.gov/2024007964
LC ebook record available at https://lccn.loc.gov/2024007965

Manufactured in the United States of America

CPSIA Compliance Information: Batch #CSWM25. For further information, contact Rosen Publishing at 1-800-237-9932

CONTENTS

Words in the glossary appear in **bold** the first time they are used in the text.

THAT'S CHEESY!

What happened when the cheese was upset?

IT HAD A MELTDOWN.

Is cheese polite?

YES, IT'S ALWAYS CURD-EOUS.

Why did the cheese get in trouble?

BECAUSE IT WAS UP TO NO GOUDA!

What did mozzarella say to cheddar?

"YOU LOOK SHARP!"

FUN FACT!

A cheese curd is cheese that isn't aged. In Canada, people eat cheese curds on top of fries in a dish called poutine.

CORNY JOKES

What kinds of jokes do vegetables like?

CORNY ONES.

What do vegetables play in the summertime?

CORNHOLE.

How do vegetables express their love?

"I LOVE YOU FROM MY HEAD TO-MA-TOES."

Why do carrots make great detectives?

THEY GET TO THE ROOT OF THE CASE.

FUN FACT!

Root vegetables are the parts of plants that are underground that people eat, such as turnips and carrots.

A DELICIOUS MIX!

What happens when you cross a cow with an earthquake?

A MILKSHAKE!

What happens when you cross a snake with dessert?

YOU GET A PIE-THON!

What do you get when you cross a ghost and a fruit salad?

BOOBERRIES.

What do you get when you cross a shellfish and fruit?

A CRAB APPLE.

FUN FACT!

Crab apples are miniature, or small-sized, apples that grow on crab apple trees in **temperate** areas of North America and Asia.

THAT'S SWEET!

What happens when berries get together to play music?

A JAM SESSION.

What's a deer's favorite ice cream?

COOKIE DOE.

Why was the cookie sent home from school?

IT WAS FEELING CRUMBY.

Why did the kid eat his quiz?

HIS TEACHER SAID IT WAS A PIECE OF CAKE.

FUN FACT!

The chocolate chip cookie is said to have been invented in 1938 by Ruth Wakefield who ran the Toll House restaurant in Whitman, Massachusetts.

FOOD FEELINGS

Why was the cheese sad?

IT WAS FEELING A LITTLE BLEU.

Why was the cheese smiling?

IT WAS FEELING GOUDA!

Why was the tomato embarrassed?

IT SAW THE SALAD DRESSING.

What did the pecan say to the walnut?

I THINK WE'RE BOTH NUTS.

FUN FACT!

Bleu cheese gets its blue color from mold that is used in it.

GROSS!

Why did the soup call the plumber?

IT HAD A LEEK.

Do pods poop?

NO, THEY ONLY PEA!

Why did the peach take a bath?

TO FRESHEN UP ITS PITS.

How many rotten eggs does it take to stink up a refrigerator?

QUITE A PHEW!

FUN FACT!

Peaches are stone fruits, a kind of fruit with a hard stone inside called a pit.

SILLY SITUATIONS

What did the police officer say when he stopped the cheese thief?

"THAT IS NACHO CHEESE!"

What did the spaghetti call the zucchini noodle?

AN IMPASTA!

What did the wheat bread say to the rye bread when they had a fight?

"YOU'RE TOAST!"

Why did the noodle run away screaming?

IT WAS AFRAID-O!

FUN FACT!

An Italian chef named Alfredo di Lelio invented creamy white alfredo sauce in 1908.

SMART FOOD

Do computers eat food?

ONLY COMPUTER CHIPS.

What did the smartphone say when she was invited to lunch?

"I'LL GRAB A BYTE."

What do astronauts eat before going to space?

LAUNCH MEAT.

Why did the yogurt go to the art museum?

TO GET SOME CULTURE.

FUN FACT!

Yogurt cultures are the bacteria that ferment the sugar in milk to make yogurt.

FUNNY FRUITS

How do bananas show their **appreciation?**

THEY SAY, "THANKS A BUNCH!"

What did the blueberry say to its friend?

"I'M BERRY FOND OF YOU."

What did the fruit say to his mom?

"YOU'RE PRETTY GRAPE!"

Why did the fruit dress up?

IT HAD A DATE.

FUN FACT!

Date palm trees have been grown by humans for up to 6,000 years in the Middle East.

GLOSSARY

appreciation: Being thankful for something.

byte: A basic unit of information in computers.

culture: The quality of knowing and caring about art, literature, good manners, and what goes on in the world.

embarrassed: Feeling uncomfortable because of shame or having too much attention from others.

express: To make thoughts and feelings known.

ferment: To cause food or drink to undergo a certain chemical change.

launch: To send into the air with great force.

leek: A plant related to the onion.

museum: A building where collections of objects that are important to history, art, or science are kept and shown to the public.

temperate: Not too hot or too cold.

FOR MORE INFORMATION

BOOKS

Rosenberg, Pam. *Food Jokes.* Parker, CO: The Child's World, 2024.

Royston, Angela. *Eat Healthy Food.* London, UK: Franklin Watts, 2024.

Thompson, Kim. *True Facts on Food.* St. Catharines, ON: Crabtree Publishing, 2023.

WEBSITES

Chew on This
kids.nationalgeographic.com/chew-on-this
Enjoy the food facts and recipes found on this helpful website.

Fun Food Facts for Kids
www.growingplay.com/2023/05/fun-food-facts-for-kids/
Learn some fascinating facts about food.

Publisher's note to educators and parents: Our editors have carefully reviewed these websites to ensure that they are suitable for students. Many websites change frequently, however, and we cannot guarantee that a site's future contents will continue to meet our high standards of quality and educational value. Be advised that students should be closely supervised whenever they access the internet.

INDEX